AF647744

(H)all Of Fear

(H)all Of Fear

Aanya Nayar

Qurate
qauratebooks.com

(H)all of Fear
Aanya Nayar

© Aanya Nayar

Published in 2025

© Published by

Qurate Books Pvt. Ltd.
Goa 403523, India
www.quratebooks.com
Tel: 1800-210-6527, Email: info@quratebooks.com

All rights reserved
No part of this publication may be reproduced, stored in a retrieval system, or transmitted in any form or by any means, electronic, mechanical, photocopying, recording or otherwise, without the prior permission of the author.

ISBN: 978-93-58984-85-9

PREFACE

This work stands as a testament to the journey my elder daughter, Aanya, has undertaken to overcome her fears, inspired by her idol, Dr. Puja Waalia Mann. I am deeply grateful to Dr. Mann for her exceptional ability to address the concerns of each student fortunate enough to be her mentee, a quality that is truly rare.

ANMOL SINGH NAYAR
Former Metropolitan Magistrate, Delhi
Former Chief Judicial Magistrate, Haryana

SOUL OF INSPIRATION:

This book is dedicated to my parents, whose unwavering love and selfless support have been my constant source of strength. It is particularly because of my father that I find myself able to craft this work today. They have always been my pillars, dispelling the shadows of fear that haunted me and shaping me into the person I am today.

I am deeply grateful to them for standing by me, especially in moments when others chose to walk away.

Introduction:

Fear takes many forms in life, and if left unchecked, it creates a fertile ground where the seeds of anxiety grow into full-blown phobias, silently taking root and holding us back. These phobias, in turn, become the shackles that tether our aspirations and dreams, hindering the boundless flight of our imagination.

Friends and acquaintances are often quick to offer advice when fears surface in conversation. While their suggestions may come in abundance, they rarely touch the deeper chords necessary to truly calm the mind and body. Over the years, I have encountered various fears, but one in particular stood out as the most significant and daunting of my life.

My parents were a constant pillar of support, but there's a limit to how long they could shield me from my struggles. I endured this fear for what felt like an eternity. Yet, as someone wisely said, "There was never a night that could defeat the sunrise." One day, I encountered a person who didn't question my fear but became a guiding light, helping me break free from it.

This story is about that fear and the journey of overcoming it. The person who transformed my fear into strength was none other than my school Principal, Dr. Puja Waalia Mann, of Pratap Public School, Karnal. Her approach was so seamless and compassionate that I hardly noticed when my dread of school transformed into sheer joy. I found myself immersed in a world of calm, balance, and peace, relishing the experience of school in ways I never thought possible.

Never
give up.
Meta AI

Fear' is a sense of despair that lingers like a dark cloud, blocking out the sun. It feels like walking on a tightrope. The first day of school can be a daunting experience for students of all ages. Whether it's entering kindergarten, transitioning to middle school, or starting college, the unknown often evokes feelings of anxiety and fear. This phenomenon is common among millions of students worldwide.

Meta AI

With my father serving as a judge in the Haryana judiciary, our family moved to a new city every 2-3 years due to his periodic transfers. Each relocation meant starting afresh in a new school, a process that often left me feeling despondent and disheartened. Walking into a new school always felt like trying to fit a mismatched puzzle piece into place.

Mornings were the hardest. When my parents dropped me off at the school gates, an overwhelming heaviness would settle over me, anchoring me down. The sight of the unfamiliar building and the thought of facing new faces triggered a throbbing heartache that seemed relentless.

Teachers and the school Principal often suggested that my parents arrange for me to travel in the school van, believing that my emotional struggles might negatively impact other students. This became a recurring pattern, and I frequently faced their disapproving reactions. People around me urged me to "stay strong" and "stop crying like a child," but no one guided me on how to achieve that.

I felt shattered and out of place. The unfamiliar hallways of each new school deepened my sadness. Everything felt alien—the classrooms, the teachers, the students. I longed for the familiarity of my previous school, where every corner held memories and every face was reassuringly familiar.

Most of all, I missed my friends. They were more than just companions; they were a part of me, and the distance between us felt unbearable. I often wondered if I would ever feel at home in these new surroundings or if I was destined to remain a puzzle piece that didn't quite fit.

Meta AI

For nine years of my childhood, I cried endlessly because of my fear of going to school. My dad often comforted me with his words: "The only constant in life is change." Those words stayed with me, and over time, I understood their depth.

My journey with school began when my dad was posted in Rewari, a district in Haryana. I struggled immensely to adjust, but the harder I tried, the more alienated I felt. For five to six years, I remained caught in this whirlwind of discomfort and fear.

Sensing my struggles, my mom decided to take up a teaching position at my school, Delhi Public School, Sirsa. Her presence brought a sense of security, and I slowly started shedding the weight of my worries. Those two years turned out to be the most blissful days of my life—I felt like I was on cloud nine.

Everything changed during that time. My heart finally found peace after what felt like an eternity. I made new friends, actively participated in various activities, and even won prizes and awards. My time with friends became a treasure trove of cherished memories—laughing together, sharing stories, and creating moments that would forever shape me.

Through it all, I discovered the joy, support, and sense of belonging that true friendship brings.

After 3 years, it was time for change, again. I took admission in Indus Public School, Jind but things were not the same as we got transferred at the time of pandemic (Coronavirus). So, I was homeschooled for a year. I used to attend online classes, sitting at home in my comfort zone. I had no fear as neither the school walls nor the teachers asked me about my identity. I was elated and enjoying my homeschooling but after some time, the government ordered the reopening of schools everywhere.

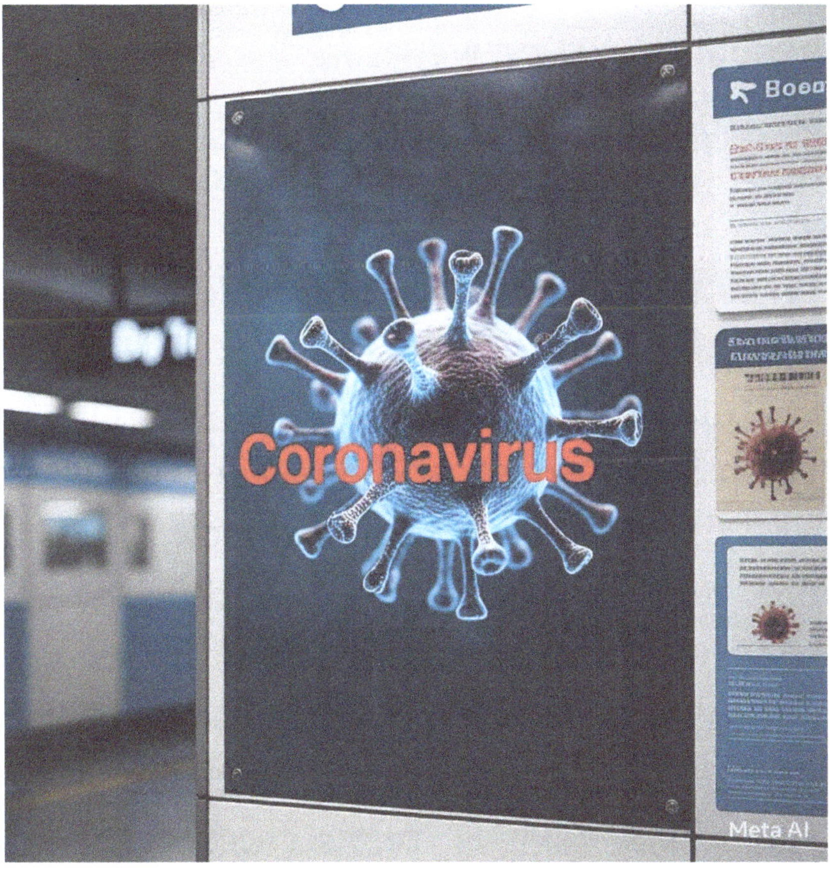
Coronavirus
Meta AI

My life's journey took a familiar turn, but this time my mom wasn't with me. Luckily, my sister Anaisha had grown up, and we both took admission to the same school. Now, we were on the same road together. I had to grow up for my sister, but a sense of "déjà vu" emerged.

Life moved on, and after some time, we shifted to Karnal. I got admitted to Pratap Public School, Karnal, in 2024. With great courage, I entered my class. The first day of school somehow passed, but on the second day, I didn't feel like going. Despite my reluctance, my parents insisted that I should get ready for school. As soon as I stepped onto the school campus, tears started rolling down my cheeks.

I tried my best to hide my emotions from everyone, but I couldn't. One of the teachers noticed and told me to go to the Principal's office, as she had seen me crying. In her office, the Principal ma'am made me sit down to comfort me. She talked to me kindly, her soothing words felt like a melody, until I started smiling. Her presence felt like a shield against life's challenges.

To reassure me, she asked if I could meet her again during recess. That small gesture made me feel cared for and valued. I felt my best in her presence. Her supportive shoulder helped me overcome my childhood fear of school. Looking back, that day marked the end of my fear of school.

Since then, my thoughts have transformed. Now, I enjoy school immensely. I walk through the gates with vivid excitement buzzing in my chest, ready to embrace another day filled with laughter and learning.

Our classroom has become a hub of creativity, brimming with colorful charts and lively discussions. Even the walls seem to greet me with a smile, welcoming me into a space where every day feels like an adventure.

Meta AI

"School is now more than just a place to learn; it has become my second home. It feels as though a switch has been flipped, and everything suddenly became more vibrant and exciting. The classrooms, once dull and daunting, have transformed into hubs of discovery and creativity. My teachers' words spark curiosity, and my classmates' laughter has become music to my ears. Recess is no longer just a break but a chance to make unforgettable memories. I have begun to see learning as an adventure, not a chore. Every subject, every activity, and every conversation has become an opportunity to grow and explore. School has become my second home, where I have found my tribe and discovered the joy of learning.

I feel that the sole credit for this transformation goes to my respected

Principal ma'am, Dr. Puja Waalia Mann. Since the day I met her, I have been enjoying everything related to my school. Even the thought of it brings a smile to my face. It feels like I have landed on my feet again. :)"

Meta AI

A poem for Principal ma'am

In every smile, and every tear,
You're present, always drawing near.
A maestro conducting life's grand symphony,
Your love orchestrates harmony.

Thank you, dear principal, for all you do,
For loving me, and seeing me through.
Your heart beats for every student, with kindness true,
A love that inspires, and forever shines anew.

Thank you so much ma'am for everything you have done to change my thoughts.

Meta AI

ABOUT THE AUTHOR:-

Aanya Nayar is a young author of 13 years, studying in class 8th in Pratap Public School, Sector -6, Karnal.

She has shared her feelings about "FEAR".

This book will help you know more about "FEAR" and how it affects one detrimentally.

WRITE YOUR OWN EXPERIENCE ABOUT FEAR, HOW YOU BROKE FREE FROM IT AND WHO HELPED YOU IN DOING SO!

DRAW YOUR PORTRAIT WHILE YOU WERE FACING OF ANY KIND!

GLOSSARY

1. **BREAK FREE-**

Break free means to escape from something.

2. **NOTIFY-**

Notify means to inform someone or give notice to.

3. **DEMATERIALIZED-**

Dematerialized refers to causing something to become or appear immaterial.

4. **DESPAIR-**

Despair means feeling that there is no hope.

5. **LINGER-**

Linger means to remain.

6. **DAUNTING-**

Daunting refers to making you feel slightly worried about your ability or to achieve something.

7. **TRANSITIONING-**

Transitioning means moving from one place to another.

8. **EVOKE-**

Evoke refers to call up or produce memories, feelings or emotions.

9. GLOOMY-

Gloomy means unpleasantly dark.

10. DISHEARTENED-

Disheartened means having lost confidence, hope or energy.

11. ANCHORING-

Anchoring refers to holding fast by or as if by an anchor.

12. THROBBING-

Throbbing means strong, regular beat or pain felt in a series of regular pulse.

13. SHATTERED-

Shattered means impaired or destroyed.

14. DISTORTED-

Distorted means twisted, misshapen or deformed.

15. SHEDDING-

Shedding means the act of getting rid of something you don't need.

16. CHERISH-

Cherish means to love, care for someone or something that is very important to you.

17. ELATED-

Elated means extremely happy or excited.

18. "DÉJÀ VU"-

"DÉJÀ VU" refers to the feeling of having experienced a situation before.

19. Shield-

Shield means to protect, to defend.

20. Vividly-

Vividly means extremely brightly or intensely.

21. Buzzing-

Buzzing means a humming sound.

22. Curiosity-

Curiosity means eager to know or learn something.

23. Chore-

Chore refers to a job or piece of work that is often boring or unpleasant but needs to be done regularly.

24. Maestro-

Maestro refers to someone who is very skilled at playing or conducting music.

25. Symphony-

Symphony means a long piece of music usually in for parts and played by an orchestra.

26. Orchestrates-

Orchestrates refers to arranging or writing a piece of music so that it can be played by an orchestra.

27. Harmony-

Harmony refers to peaceful existence or agreement.

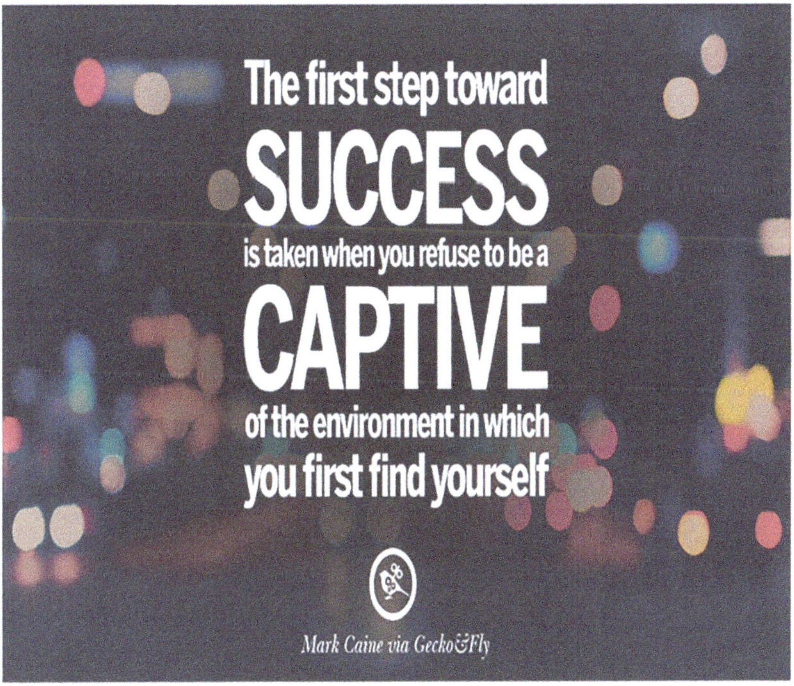
The first step toward
SUCCESS
is taken when you refuse to be a
CAPTIVE
of the environment in which
you first find yourself
Mark Caine via Gecko&Fly